LET'S Bake a cake

LET'S Bake a Cake

RECIPES *from* THE GOLDEN AGE OF BAKING

BENJAMIN DARLING

LAUGHING ELEPHANT MMXIII

ISBN: 978-1-59583-625-0

LAUGHING ELEPHANT

LAUGHINGELEPHANT.COM

Table of Contents

Introduction

Qu'ils mangent de la brioche!

"Let Them Eat Cake!" Marie Antoinette (perhaps) quipped when she was told that the French peasantry was out of (French?) bread. The sheer cheek of her remark, as she presumably gamboled about Versailles amply supplied with cake, is emblematic even to this day of indifference, and also very indicative of the high regard in which cake was held. The chasm between Marie's glorious gateau, torte and brioche-filled existence and that of the common bread-eating citizen was, in the end, too great for the masses to bear in fraternité.

Ms. Antoinette chose cake and not pudding, or s'mores, or Eskimo pies (all of which she doubtless had on hand) because cake has the potential to be the most decadent of all desserts. Cake alone has an architectural quality that naturally leads to elaborate indulgence in both basic form and ornamentation. Additionally, cake's natural state, and yumminess, can be aggrandized with sumptuous ingredients and additions - in it, between its layers, and all over its surface. The wealth and baroque intricacies that can be lavished upon cake are seemingly limitless; that is, at least, until the revolution...

How to make Tempting Nutritious Desserts, 1941

Cake is artistic in form; it is both a clay to be sculpted and a canvas to be painted upon. In form a cake can be a pirate ship, a teddy bear, an American flag, or even an elaborately decorated object, within the specific vocabulary of 'cakeness' itself. A cake can be tall and impossibly cantilevered to the point of wonderment, or it can be square and solid like a frosted mausoleum, paying dignified homage to whatever or whomever it has been made for. The frequently inedible gingerbread house is an attempt by the quotidian cookie to reach cake-like heights. In its adornment, cake, again unlike any other dessert, is only confined by the limits of artistic imagination.

One can paint a cake with icing just as one paints a painting with oils. Portraits of loved ones and historical figures can be painted on cakes, (and then eaten?!), landscape cakes of scenes both pastoral and fantastical can be pleasing to both the eyes and the stomach. Abstract art lends itself very aptly to the cake; Joan Miró could just as well have been a cake decorator.

One can also write upon cakes, and one of the oldest and most common uses for the cake, is the message cake: Happy Birthday, Bon Voyage, or what you will; the cake communicates the desires of the giver and perhaps the group, which is then symbolically eaten. What other food can claim that dual role of both messenger and meal? The Fortune Cookie is a poor substitute in which not even the message is edible.

The basic cake can have a variety of icings and toppings– it can be substantial and filling like a pound cake or fruit cake, or it can be light as a feather, a melt-on-your-tongue moment like a an angel food cake. The basic cakes featured in this book are plain, chocolate and spice. There are an infinitude of variations on this theme, but these are three good pillars upon which to build our understanding of cakes, much as red, yellow and blue are to the colors. The fillings, frostings and additions to cake are also as limitless as the imagination, but again there are a few themes upon which we can build Antoinette-like chocolate icing, white or butter cream icing, and the caramel and meringue-based icings; all the basic icings and fillings can be flavored with vanilla, almond, rosewater, citrus and an infinitude of other spices and flavorings. A great part of the fun of cake-making is joining cake, filling and frosting flavors and finding new combinations.

So Marie Antoinette, though probably vapid and uncaring, and yes, ultimately guillotined, was correct in her assertion that cake was and is the ne plus ultra of desserts. Let us all eat cake!

About the Author

Benjamin Darling is an author and publisher who, together with his family, manages The Laughing Elephant, a publisher of books and gift products celebrating the ideals and illustrations of the past. He has been collecting recipe booklets for some twenty years, ever since he found a small collection of them at an estate sale and admired the color illustrations of cakes and pies and casseroles.

The Basic Cakes

The world is so full of different cake recipes that it helps to know there are really only two kinds of cakes. Butter Cakes, also known as "shortened" cakes, are so named because they are made with butter or some shortening. They use leavening, like baking powder, to make them light. These cakes include the fudge cakes, white cakes, spice cakes, pound cakes, and so on—cakes that are always favorites.

Butter cakes can be made in two ways—the mix-easy way or by the regular creaming method.

Sponge Cakes are usually made without shortening and are often leavened just by air beaten into eggs. These cakes include sponge cakes, jellyroll, even angel food, and chiffon cake, newest of all.

Plenty of famous cake makers have won a glowing reputation with just one of these cakes! So don't think you must learn them all at once.

Just start with a cake that seems easy to you and you'll soon be ready and eager to try other recipes like it. Then switch to a different type. Before long you'll be making any cake you fancy!

The Basic Frostings

Frostings, too, for all their seeming variety, usually divide into only four basic types: seven-minute frostings, the short-cut boiled frostings made by beating the ingredients over boiling water in a double boiler; easy, never-fail uncooked butter frostings, the most used kind; cooked frostings that taste like dreamy fondant candy and fluffy boiled frostings made by beating a boiled syrup into egg white. As with cake, just start with a simple frosting and work up. In this book you'll find plenty of good frosting ideas.

SEVEN MINUTE FROSTING

Here's one of the easiest cooked frostings. With a deep double boiler, a good hand eggbeater or electric beater, Seven Minute is almost as simple and quick as uncooked frosting. It's fluffy, delicious, and lavish looking. All through the book are excellent variations to try.

UNCOOKED BUTTER FROSTING

Quick, easy, can't fail, and long keeping—this is the kind of frosting to learn early and make frequently. It consists of confectioners' sugar beaten with butter or margarine (or cream cheese). A little milk or juice is added, and flavoring!

QUICK COOKED FROSTING

Luscious, long-keeping frostings are made by cooking milk with granulated sugar, then thickening with confectioners' sugar.

BOILED FROSTING

This much-prized frosting piles up fluffy and high, with a fine gloss. It is a little more difficult for beginners. Boiled frosting is made by cooking a sugar syrup until exactly right and beating it slowly into beaten egg whites. A candy thermometer helps get extra good results. Try this frosting after you have mastered the other kinds.

Monarch White Cake

INGREDIENTS

2⁄3 cups sifted cake flour
1¼ cups sugar
½ tsp. salt
1 cup butter or shortening
2¼ tsp. baking powder
1 tsp. vanilla extract
4 egg whites

WHITE MOUNTAIN CREAM

1½ cups sugar
2 egg whites, stiffly beaten
½ tsp. light corn syrup
1 tsp. vanilla extract
2⁄3 cup boiling water
¼ tsp. orange extract

DIRECTIONS

Preheat oven to 325°F

Sift flour once, measure, add baking powder and salt, and sift together. Cream butter thoroughly, add sugar gradually, and cream together until light and fluffy. Add vanilla. Add egg whites, one at a time, and beat until thoroughly blended. Add flour, alternately with water, a small amount at a time. Beat after each addition until smooth. Turn into two deep, greased 9-inch layer pans. Bake in moderate oven (325°F.) 10 minutes; then increase heat slightly (375°F.) and bake 20 minutes longer, or until done. Cool thoroughly. Put layers together and cover top and sides of cake with White Mountain Cream.

WHITE MOUNTAIN CREAM

Combine sugar, corn syrup, and water in a saucepan. Bring quickly to a boil, stirring only until sugar is dissolved. Boil rapidly, without stirring, until a small amount of syrup forms a soft ball in cold water, or spins a long thread when dropped from tip of spoon (240°F.) Pour syrup in fine stream over egg whites beating constantly with whisk. Add flavoring. Continue beating 10 to 15 minutes, or until frosting is cool and of consistency to spread.

Magazine advertisement, 1931.

Cream Cake

INGREDIENTS

3 cups cake flour
3 tsp. baking powder
3 eggs, separated
¾ cup cold water
½ cup butter
1¼ cups granulated sugar
1 tsp. orange extract

FILLING
1 whole egg
1 teaspoon cinnamon, nutmeg and ½ teaspoon cloves
1 teaspoon vanilla extract
1 tablespoon cream or milk
2 cups confectioners' sugar

DIRECTIONS

Sift flour once, then measure; add baking powder and sift; cream butter and sugar, add the well beaten yolks, then flour and water alternately, then extract, beat long and hard and fold in lightly the well beaten whites. Bake in 375°F oven for 30 to 35 minutes. Cool thoroughly.

FILLING
Put into deep bowl the egg, vanilla, milk and spices, add sugar gradually, beating long and hard. Spread on cake when cool.

Orange Bonbon Cake

INGREDIENTS

¾ cup butter or shortening
1 tsp. salt
Grated rind of 1 orange
1½ cups sugar 3 eggs
3 tsp. baking powder
3 cups sifted flour
Juice of 1 medium sized orange
2 tbs. lemon juice Water

BONBON FROSTING

2 tsp. orange rind
5 tbs. orange juice
3 tbs. butter
¼ tsp. salt
2½ cups sifted confectioners' sugar
1½ oz. chocolate, melted
1 tbs. cream (approx.)

DIRECTIONS

Preheat oven to 375°F.

Blend butter, salt, and grated orange rind. Add sugar gradually and cream well. Add eggs singly, beating thoroughly after each addition. Sift baking powder with flour. Combine orange juice and lemon juice and add water to make 1 cup. Add flour to creamed mixture, alternately with combined fruit juices and water, mixing after each addition until smooth. Bake in two greased 9-inch layer pans, 25 to 30 minutes. Cool. Spread Bonbon Frosting between layers and on top of cake.

BONBON FROSTING

Let orange rind stand in orange juice 10 minutes; strain. Cream butter, and salt together. Add ½ cup sugar gradually, creaming until light and fluffy. Add chocolate and blend. Add remaining sugar, alternately with orange juice, beating until smooth. Add ½ cream and beat well. Add just enough cream to make a nice spreading consistency, using more or less as necessary.

Orange Cream Cake

INGREDIENTS

3 cups sifted cake flour
1½ cups sugar
3 tsp. baking powder
1 cup milk
½ cup butter or shortening
½ tsp. lemon extract
4 egg whites, stiffly beaten

ORANGE FILLING

½ cup sugar
4 tbs. cake flour
3 tbs. lemon juice
2 tbs. water
Dash of salt
1 egg, well beaten
⅓ cup orange juice
2 tbs. butter
1½ tsp. grated orange rind

DIRECTIONS

Preheat oven to 375°F

Sift flour once, measure, add baking powder, and sift together. Cream butter thoroughly, add sugar gradually, and cream together until light and fluffy. Add flour, alternately with milk, a small amount at a time, beating after each addition until smooth. Add lemon extract. Fold in egg whites quickly and thoroughly. Bake in two greased 9-inch layer pans in moderate oven (375°F.) 25 to 30 minutes. Cool thoroughly.

Spread Orange Filling between layers and *White Mountain Cream* (see page 8) over cake. Decorate with orange sections.

ORANGE FILLING

Combine sugar, flour and salt in top of double boiler; add fruit juice, water and egg, mixing thoroughly. Place over rapidly boiling water and cook 10 minutes, stirring constantly. Remove from boiling water; add butter and orange rind. Cool and spread.

Prize Orange Coconut Cake

DIRECTIONS

Preheat oven to 350°F
Cream butter and sugar. Add egg yolks and orange zest, blend together. Add dry ingredients, which have been sifted together in three additions, alternately with orange juice and water in two additions.
Beat just enough to make batter smooth.
Blend in coconut. Fold in egg whites.
Pour into three 9-inch cake pans, greased and floured. Bake 30 minutes in moderate oven (350° F.). Cool thoroughly.

Put layers together with Prize Orange Filling and cover with Orange Frosting. Sprinkle with: ¾ cup moist, shredded coconut. Decorate with orange segments.

PRIZE ORANGE FILLING (Sufficient for 1 cake)
Mix smooth in double boiler:

2 tbs. flour
4 level tbs. cornstarch
1 cup sugar
½ tsp. salt

Add slowly the following, stirring constantly:

⅓ cup orange juice
3 tbs. lemon juice
¼ cup water

ADD: 2 tsp. butter
Grated rind 1 orange

Cook over boiling water, stirring occasionally until thick (about 20 minutes). Cool. Spread between layers of cake.

ORANGE FROSTING (Sufficient for 1 cake)
Put in double boiler. Beat constantly while cooking over boiling water 6 to 7 minutes. Remove from heat; add ½ tsp. lemon juice and sprinkling of salt. Beat thoroughly and spread on cake.

INGREDIENTS

¾ cup butter or shortening
2 cups sugar
1½ tsp. grated orange rind
2 egg yolks
3¼ cups cake flour
4½ tsp. baking powder
½ tsp. salt
½ cup orange juice
¾ cup water
½ cup moist, shredded coconut
4 egg whites, beaten stiff, not dry

ORANGE FROSTING
1 tsp. light corn syrup
⅞ cup sugar
¼ tsp. grated orange rind
1 egg white
3 tbs. orange juice

Orange Soda Layer Cake

INGREDIENTS

1 box white cake mix
Orange soda
(substitute for water
called for in cake directions)
Eggs & Oil (see cake directions)
Grated rind of 1 orange

ORANGE SODA CREAMY FROSTING
½ cup butter
3 cups sifted confectioners sugar
¼ tsp. salt
4 tbs. flour.
⅔ cup orange soda pop

DIRECTIONS

Preheat oven to 350°F

Mix cake as directed, substituting orange soda for water. Fold in orange rind. Bake in 2 greased 9 inch cake pans at time and temperature directed on package. Cool thoroughly.

ORANGE SODA CREAMY FROSTING
Melt shortening in heavy saucepan. Remove from heat, blend in flour and salt, into a roux. Stirring constantly add orange soda, slowly beating to keep smooth.

Return to low heat and bring to gentle boil. Cook one minute, stirring.

Remove from heat, add sugar at once beating well. Set saucepan in basin of cold water and continue to beat until of spreading consistency

Recipes With Nesbitt's, n.d.

Chocolate Topper Cake

INGREDIENTS

1/3 cup butter or shortening
3/4 tsp. salt
1 tsp. vanilla extract
1 cup sugar
1 egg, unbeaten
2½ tsp. baking powder
2 cups sifted flour
3/4 cup milk

CHOCOLATE TOPPER
8-oz. bar semisweet chocolate
1 cup whipping cream

DIRECTIONS

Preheat oven to 375°F

Blend butter, salt, and vanilla. Add sugar gradually and cream well. Add egg and beat. Sift baking powder with flour. Add to creamed mixture, alternately with milk, mixing after each addition until smooth. Bake in oblong 12 x 8-inch greased pan in moderate oven (375°F.) 30 to 35 minutes. Cool in pan. When cool, spread Chocolate Topper on top of cake and serve in squares.

CHOCOLATE TOPPER
Melt one 7 or 8-oz. bar semisweet or bittersweet chocolate; cool. Fold into 1 cup cream (whipped) very lightly to give a mottled effect.

Plantation Crunch Cake

INGREDIENTS

½ cup butter or shortening
¾ tsp. salt
1 tsp. vanilla extract
1 cup brown sugar, firmly packed
2 eggs, unbeaten
2½ tsp. baking powder
2 cups sifted flour
¾ cup milk

PEANUT CRUNCH
4 tbs. butter
½ cup brown sugar, firmly packed
2 tbs. cream
1 cup peanuts, chopped

DIRECTIONS

Blend butter, salt, and vanilla. Add sugar gradually and cream well. Add eggs, singly, beating well after each addition. Sift baking powder with flour. Add flour to creamed mixture, alternately with milk, mixing after each addition until smooth. Bake in greased 10 x 10 x 2-inch pan in moderate oven (350°F.) 40 to 45 minutes. While cake is baking, prepare Peanut Crunch.

PEANUT CRUNCH
Combine butter, brown sugar, and cream in saucepan and bring to a boil. Remove from fire and add nuts. Pour on warm cake and spread evenly. Place cake low under low broiler and broil slowly until nuts are slightly toasted. Makes enough icing to cover top of 10 x 10-inch loaf.

Coconut Layer Cake

INGREDIENTS

2 cups sifted cake flour
2 tsp. baking powder
½ tsp. salt
⅔ cup butter or shortening
1½ cups sugar
3 eggs
⅔ cup milk
1 tsp. vanilla extract

SEVEN MINUTE FROSTING
2 egg whites, unbeaten
1½ cups sugar
5 tbs. water
1½ tsp. light corn syrup
1 tsp. vanilla extract
red food coloring, as needed
coconut, to cover cake

DIRECTIONS

Preheat oven to 375°F

Sift flour once, measure, add baking powder and salt, and sift together. Cream butter, add sugar gradually, and cream together until light and fluffy. Beat eggs until very thick and light; add to creamed mixture and beat well. Add flour, alternately with milk, a small amount at a time, beating after each addition until smooth. Add vanilla. Bake in two greased 9-inch layer pans in moderate oven (375°F.) about 25 minutes. Cool. Spread Seven Minute Frosting tinted a delicate shell pink, between layers and on top and sides of cake. Sprinkle with coconut while frosting is still soft.

SEVEN MINUTE FROSTING
Combine egg whites, sugar, water, and corn syrup in top of double boiler, beating until thoroughly mixed. Place over rapidly boiling water, beat constantly, and cook 7 minutes, or until frosting will stand in peaks. Remove from boiling water; add vanilla and beat until thick enough to spread. Tint lightly with food coloring.

Lemon Coconut Cake

INGREDIENTS

2 cups sifted cake flour
1 tsp. vanilla extract
3 tsp. baking powder
5 egg whites
½ tsp. salt
½ cup butter
1½ cups sugar
⅔ cup milk
Shredded coconut to cover cake

LEMON FILLING
½ cup sugar
¼ cup flour
1 cup warm water
3 well beaten egg yolks
Juice & grated peel of 1 lemon
2 tbs. butter

FLUFFY WHITE FROSTING
1 cup sugar
⅓ cup water
1 tsp. vinegar
2 egg whites
½ tsp. vanilla extract

DIRECTIONS

Preheat oven to 375°F

Grease and flour two 8-inch round cake pans. Sift together flour, baking powder, and salt. Cream shortening and sugar until fluffy. Combine milk and vanilla. Add alternately with flour mixture to sugar mixture. Whip egg whites until stiff; fold into flour mixture. Spoon into pans. Bake 25 to 30 minutes; or until brown. Cool in pans 5 minutes. Remove and cool on a rack. Spread filling between layers. Cover top and sides with frosting and sprinkle generously with coconut.

LEMON FILLING Mix together ½ cup sugar and ¼ cup flour; gradually add 1 cup warm water. Stir in 3 well beaten egg yolks. Cook over hot water until thick, stirring constantly. Cover; cook 5 minutes longer. Remove from heat, add juice and grated peel of 1 lemon and 2 tablespoons; butter or margarine; mix well. Cool thoroughly.

FLUFFY WHITE FROSTING Combine 1 cup sugar, 1 /3 cup water, and 1 teaspoon vinegar in a saucepan. Place over moderate heat; stir until sugar dissolves. Boil without stirring to 236°F. on a candy thermometer or until syrup spins a thread when dropped from the tip of a spoon. Whip 2 egg whites until stiff but not dry. Pour hot syrup slowly on egg whites, beating constantly. Continue beating until frosting holds its shape. Stir in ½ teaspoon vanilla.

Cakes Men Like, 1955

Feather Coconut Cake

INGREDIENTS

1½ cups flour
1 egg
7/8 cup sugar
½ cup milk
4 tsp. Baking Powder
1 tsp. lemon extract
4 tbs. melted butter or shortening
½ cup grated coconut

DIRECTIONS

Preheat oven to 375°F

Sift together flour, sugar and baking powder. Add melted shortening and beaten egg to milk and add to dry ingredients. Mix well; add flavoring and coconut and bake in greased and floured loaf pan in moderate oven at 375°F. thirty-five to forty-five minutes. Cool thoroughly. Sprinkle with powdered sugar or cover with any icing desired.

Makes one seven-inch loaf

Anyone Can Bake, 1927

Sungold Coconut Cake

INGREDIENTS

2 cups sugar
1 cup butter or shortening
4 eggs, separated
1 cup milk
3 cups cake flour
3 tsp. baking powder
1 tsp. vanilla extract;
½ tsp. salt

COCONUT CREAM ICING

1 package coconut (7 oz.)
2 cups confectioners' sugar
4 tbs. heavy cream
½ tsp. vanilla extract.

DIRECTIONS

Preheat oven to 375°F

Beat the butter and sugar to a smooth cream. Stir in the well-beaten egg yolks and beat well. Sift dry ingredients together and add alternately with milk to first mixture. Add vanilla and carefully fold in the whites of the eggs which have been beaten to a stiff froth. Bake in layers in a moderate oven 375° Cool thoroughly.

COCONUT CREAM ICING

Put the sugar in a bowl, add the cream a little at a time and beat steadily. Add Vanilla. When the icing is the right consistency, spread over the top of the layers and sprinkle heavily with coconut. Put together and ice sides, covering with coconut.

Magazine advertisement, 1925.

Nun's Cake

INGREDIENTS

1 cup butter
1½ cups powdered sugar
Yolks of 5 eggs
Whites of 2 eggs
¾ cup milk
3 cups pastry flour
2½ tsp. baking powder
3 tsp. caraway seeds
¼ tsp. salt
1 tsp. rose extract
  or rosewater
1 tsp. cinnamon

DIRECTIONS

Preheat oven to 325°F

Beat butter until soft and creamy; add sugar and yolks of eggs, beating well. Stir in unbeaten whites of eggs and beat one minute. Sift flour with baking powder and salt and add alternately, a little at a time with milk. Mix well but do not beat. Sprinkle in caraway seeds, cinnamon and rosewater; mix well. Pour into well-greased and floured loaf pan and bake one hour and forty minutes in moderate oven at 325°F. Makes one loaf about 7½″ in diameter and 3½″ high

Maple Syrup Cake

INGREDIENTS

½ cup butter or shortening
2½ cups cake flour
½ cup granulated sugar
2 eggs, beaten light
⅔ tsp. baking soda
1 cup maple syrup
2 tsp. baking powder
½ cup hot water
½ tsp. ginger
walnuts, to decorate

MAPLE FROSTING

1 cup maple sugar
2 egg whites, stiffly beaten
1 tbs. corn syrup
1 tsp. vanilla extract
⅔ cup boiling water

DIRECTIONS

Preheat oven to 350°F

Cream the butter; gradually add the sugar. Add the eggs, beaten without separating the whites and yolks. Add the maple syrup, then the water alternately with the flour; which has been sifted, measured, and sifted again with the ginger, soda and baking powder added. Bake in a greased 9″ tube pan about 50 minutes. Cool thoroughly. Cover with Maple Icing and decorate with halves of English walnuts.

MAPLE FROSTING

Combine sugar, corn syrup, and water. Bring quickly to a boil, stirring only until sugar is dissolved. Boil rapidly, without stirring, until a small amount of syrup forms a soft ball in cold water, or spins a long thread when dropped from tip of spoon (240°F.) Pour syrup in fine stream over egg whites, beating constantly. Continue beating 10 to 15 minutes, or until frosting is cool and of consistency to spread.

Cake Secrets, 1922

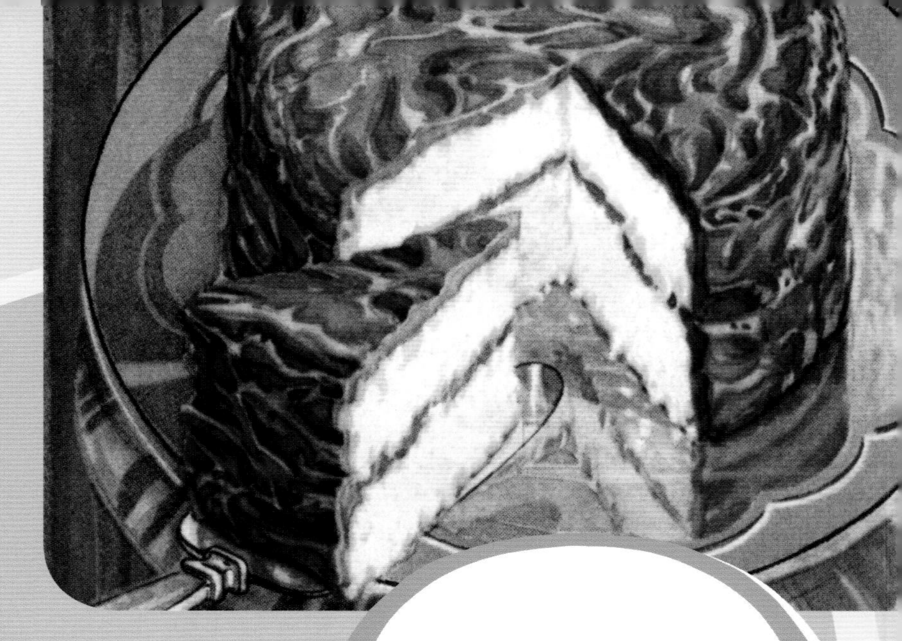

Caramel Layer Cake

INGREDIENTS

1⅔ cups sifted cake flour
1 cup sugar
1½ tsp. baking powder
2 eggs, well beaten
⅓ cup butter or shortening
½ cup milk
1 tsp. vanilla extract

CARAMEL FROSTING

1½ cups brown sugar, firmly packed
1 cup milk
½ cup granulated sugar
1 tbs. butter

DIRECTIONS

Preheat oven to 375°F

Sift flour once, measure, add baking powder, and sift together. Cream butter thoroughly, add sugar gradually, and cream together until light and fluffy. Add eggs, then flour, alternately with milk, a small amount at a time. Beat after each addition until smooth. Add vanilla. Bake in two greased 8-inch layer pans in moderate oven (375°F.) 25 minutes. Cool thoroughly. Spread Caramel Frosting between layers and on top and sides of cake.

CARAMEL FROSTING

Boil brown sugar, granulated sugar, and milk until syrup forms a soft ball in cold water (232°F.). Add butter and remove from fire. Cool to lukewarm (110°F.); beat until thick and creamy and of right consistency to spread. Makes enough frosting to cover tops and sides of two layers.

Silver Moon Cake

INGREDIENTS

2⅔ cups sifted flour
3 tsp. baking powder
1 tsp. salt
5 egg whites
½ cup sugar
⅔ cup shortening
1 tsp. vanilla extract or
grated lemon rind
1¼ cups sugar
1 cup milk

7 MINUTE FROSTING
2 egg whites, unbeaten
1½ cups sugar
5 tbs. water
1½ tsp. light corn syrup
1 tsp. vanilla extract
2 oz. unsweetened chocolate,
melted & cooled

DECORATION
1 oz. semisweet chocolate
1 teaspoon melted butter

DIRECTIONS

Preheat oven to 375°F. Sift flour once, measure, add baking powder and salt, and sift together three times. In small mixer bowl, beat egg whites at high speed until foamy. Add ¼ cup sugar gradually, beating only until meringue will hold up in soft peaks. In large mixer bowl, beat shortening and flavoring at medium speed until smooth. Turn to high speed and add ¼ cup sugar gradually during 1 minute's beating. Scrape down bowl and beater well: then beat 1 minute longer. Add flour mixture, alternately with milk in small amounts, beating at low speed after each. Add first about ¼ of flour, beat 20 seconds; then add ⅓ of milk; beat 20 seconds more. Continue rapidly in this way until all flour and milk are used. Scrape down bowl and beater. Add meringue and beat 1 minute more. Turn into two round 9-inch layer pans, 1½ inches deep, which have been lined on bottoms with paper, then greased. Bake in moderate oven (375°F.) about 30 minutes. Cool thoroughly.

7 MINUTE FROSTING Combine egg whites, sugar, water, and corn syrup in top of double boiler, beating until thoroughly mixed. Place over rapidly-boiling water, beat constantly with, and cook 7 minutes, or until frosting will stand in peaks. Remove from boiling water; add vanilla and beat until thick enough to spread. Fold in melted unsweetened chocolate. Fill and frost cake.

DECORATION Dribble over finished cake as in photo.

Peppermint BonBon Cake

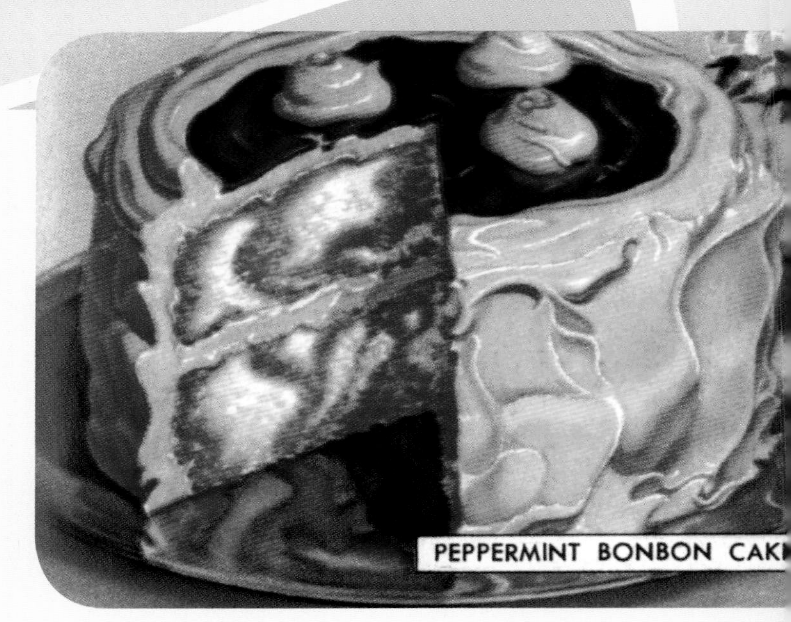
PEPPERMINT BONBON CAK

DIRECTIONS

Preheat oven to 350°F

SIFT TOGETHER:
2 cups sifted cake flour
1½ cups sugar
4 tsp. baking powder
1 tsp. salt

ADD:
½ cups butter or shortening
⅔ cup milk
½ teaspoon vanilla
Beat 2 minutes

ADD:
⅓ cup milk
Add 4 egg yolks
Beat 2 minutes

PAN SIZE: 2 round layers, 8-in. diameter, 1½ in. deep (or 9-in. diameter, 1½ in. deep)

TEMPERATURE: 350°F (moderate oven).

TIME: 30 to 35 minutes.

Tint half the batter a delicate pink with red food coloring. Pour here and there over white batter in pan. Cut through batter several times with knife for marbled effect. Frost with Fluffy White Icing flavored with peppermint oil and tinted delicate pink forming ridge around top of cake and reserving several tbs. to use later. Melt together 1 sq. (1 oz.) chocolate and ¼ tsp. shortening. Pour over top of cake keeping inside of ridge. When chocolate has set, drop small spoonfuls of pink icing on top to form 5 bonbons

FLUFFY WHITE ICING
Mix 1 cup sugar, ⅓ cup water. Boil without stirring until mixture spins 8-in. thread (242°) (Keep pan covered first 3 min.). Pour hot syrup slowly into 2 stiffly beaten egg whites (with ¼ tsp. cream of tartar added when whites are frothy). Beat constantly with rotary beater. Add 1 tsp. vanilla and peppermint oil or extract to taste. Continue beating until mixture is fluffy and will hold shape. Tint with red food coloring.

Regal Butter Cake

INGREDIENTS

2¼ cups sifted cake flour
2¼ tsp. baking powder
½ tsp. salt
⅔ cup butter (at room temp.)
1½ cups sugar
3 eggs, unbeaten
⅔ cup milk
1 tsp. vanilla extract

7 MINUTE FROSTING
2 egg whites, unbeaten
1½ cups sugar
5 tbs. water
1½ tsp. light corn syrup
1 tsp. vanilla extract
Red, green & yellow food coloring

DIRECTIONS

Preheat oven to 375°F

Use two round 9-inch layer pans, 1½ inches deep; line bottoms with paper. Sift flour before measuring.

THE MIXING METHOD Measure sifted flour, add baking powder and salt, and sift together. Cream butter, add sugar gradually, and cream together until light and fluffy. Add eggs, one at a time, beating well after each. Then add flour, alternately with the milk, in small amounts, beating after each addition until smooth. Add vanilla, blend.

BAKING Pour batter into pans. Bake in moderate oven (375°F.) about 25 minutes. Cool thoroughly.

RAINBOW FROSTING
Prepare seven minute frosting. Tint half pink. Divide rest in half and tint part yellow, part light green. Save half of the pink frosting for sides of cake. Put spoonfuls of each color frosting on top of first layer, alternating colors and spreading slightly to cover. To make rainbow, draw flat side of knife through frosting, starting at center and circling around cake. Cover with second layer and repeat rainbow effect. Spread remaining pink frosting around sides of cake.

SEVEN MINUTE FROSTING
Combine egg whites, sugar, water, and corn syrup in top of double boiler, beating until thoroughly mixed. Place over rapidly boiling water, beat constantly with rotary egg beater, and cook 7 minutes, or until frosting will stand in peaks. Remove from boiling water; add vanilla and beat until thick enough to spread.

Banana Nut Cake

INGREDIENTS

3 cups cake flour
3 tsp. baking powder
¾ cup butter
1½ cups sugar
1 cup milk
3 eggs, separated
1 tsp. vanilla extract

ICING

1½ cups brown sugar
½ cup water
2 egg whites, stiffly beaten
1 tsp. vanilla extract
½ cup finely chopped walnuts
1 banana, sliced
(use 2 bananas if small)

DIRECTIONS

Preheat oven to 375°F

Sift flour once before measuring. Mix and sift dry ingredients three times. Cream butter, add sugar gradually, then egg yolks. Beat hard until light and fluffy. Add milk and dry ingredients alternately, beating after each addition. Add vanilla and fold in stiffly beaten egg whites. Bake in two 9-inch greased pans in 375°F oven for 30 minutes or until done. Cool thoroughly.

ICING

Boil water and sugar until it spins a thread in cold water, 235°F. Remove from heat and carefully pour over egg whites, while beating. Add vanilla and continue beating until cool and creamy. Place banana slices over top of lower layer of cake and top with icing. Cover with second cake layer. Spread remainder of icing over top of cake and lightly on sides. (Nuts may be omitted if desired.)

Magazine advertisement, 1925

Lady Baltimore Cake

INGREDIENTS

3 cups sifted flour
½ cup milk
½ cup water
3 tsp. baking powder
1 tsp. vanilla extract
¼ tsp. almond flavoring
¼ tsp. salt
l/2 cup butter or shortening
3 egg whites, stiff
1½ cups sugar

LADY BALTIMORE FILLING & ICING

¼ lb. figs
½ lb. raisins
½ lb. pecans
or English walnuts
2 cups sugar
¾ cup water
2 egg whites, beaten stiff
1 tsp. vanilla extract

DIRECTIONS

Preheat oven to 375°F

Prepare pan. Sift flour once, measure, add baking powder and salt, and sift together. Cream shortening until light and fluffy, then add sugar gradually and cream together thoroughly. Add sifted dry ingredients to creamed mixture alternately with milk, a small amount at a time. Beat after each addition until smooth. Add flavorings; fold in egg whites. Bake in a moderate oven, 375 °F. from 20 to 25 minutes. Cool thoroughly.

LADY BALTIMORE FILLING & ICING

Grind fruits and nuts together. (A food processor may be used.) Cook sugar and water to soft bail stage, 238°F. Pour syrup slowly on egg whites. Beat until mixture will stand alone. Add vanilla. Stir fruits and nuts into two-thirds of icing. Spread between layers and on top of cake. Cover entire cake with remaining plain icing.

Magazine advertisement, 1927

Pineapple Upside Down Cake

INGREDIENTS

¼ cup butter
½ cup packed brown sugar
4 slices pineapple, cut in wedges
1⅓ cups sifted cake flour
2 tsp. baking powder
¼ tsp. salt
¾ cup granulated sugar
¼ cup butter or shortening
(at room temperature)
1 egg, unbeaten
½ cup milk
1 tsp. vanilla extract

DIRECTIONS

Preheat oven to 350°F

MIXING METHOD Melt butter in 8 x 8 x 2-inch square pan or 8-inch skillet. Add brown sugar; blend well. Remove from heat. Arrange pineapple wedges on sugar mixture; set aside.

Measure sifted flour, add baking powder, salt, and granulated sugar, and sift together three times. Cream shortening. Add dry ingredients, egg, milk, and vanilla. Stir until all flour is dampened, then beat vigorously 1 minute.

BAKING Pour batter over fruit mixture in pan. Bake in a moderate oven (350°F.) about 50 minutes. Cool cake in pan 5 minutes. Then invert on plate and let stand a minute before removing pan. Serving. Upside down cake is best when served warm. It may be garnished with whipped cream or a variation. It is also delicious with ice cream.

Cake Secrets, n.d.

Upside Down Butter Cakes

DIRECTIONS

PINEAPPLE SPICE UPSIDE DOWN CAKE

Try adding the surprise of spices to the pineapple favorite for a new flavor idea.

Prepare as for Pineapple Upside Down Cake, adding 1 teaspoon cinnamon, ½ teaspoon nutmeg, and ⅛ teaspoon cloves to flour mixture.

FRESH BLUEBERRY UPSIDE DOWN CAKE

Prepare as for Pineapple Upside Down Cake. For the topping, melt 3 tablespoons butter in 8 x 8 x 2-inch square pan. Add ⅓ cup firmly packed brown sugar and mix well. Pour in 1¾ cups fresh blueberries over sugar mixture; sprinkle with ½ teaspoon grated lemon rind and 2 teaspoons lemon juice.

COCONUT BUTTERSCOTCH UPSIDE DOWN CAKE

Prepare as for Pineapple Upside Down Cake. For the topping, sauté 1 cup finely cut coconut in 1 tablespoon of melted butter in 8 x 8 x 2-inch square pan until golden brown. Then add 3 tablespoons more butter, ½ cup firmly packed brown sugar, and ¼ cup water; heat until blended, stirring constantly. Serve plain or with whipped cream.

CRANBERRY UPSIDE DOWN CAKE

Use Pineapple Upside Down Cake batter.

For topping, melt 3 tablespoons butter in 8 x 8 x 2-inch square pan. Add 6 tablespoons sugar and 1 tablespoon grated orange rind; mix well. Sprinkle 1½ cups fresh cranberries, coarsely cut, over sugar mixture. Cover with batter and bake as directed.

APRICOT OR PEACH UPSIDE DOWN CAKE

Use batter for plain or spiced Pineapple Upside Down Cake. For the topping, substitute 20 cooked dried apricot halves or 12 canned apricot halves, or 1¼ cups of well drained sliced peaches for the pineapple slices in recipe. Arrange on sugar mixture. Cover with batter and bake as directed. Serve plain or with ice cream.

Individual Shortcakes

INGREDIENTS

3 cups sifted cake flour
3 tsp. baking powder
1 tsp. salt
½ cup butter or shortening
¾ cup milk
2 quarts strawberries
or other fruit

DIRECTIONS

Preheat oven to 450°F

Sift flour once, measure, add baking powder and salt, and sift again. Cut in shortening; add milk all at once and stir carefully until all flour is dampened. Then stir vigorously until mixture forms a soft dough and follows spoon around bowl. Turn out immediately on slightly floured board and knead 30 seconds. Roll ¼ inch thick and cut with 1 floured 3-inch biscuit cutter. Place half of circles on un-greased baking sheet; brush with melted butter. Place remaining circles on top and butter tops well. Bake in hot oven (450°F.) 15 to 20 minutes.

Cut berries in small pieces and sweeten slightly. Separate halves of hot shortcakes; spread bottom half with soft butter and part of strawberries. Adjust top and spread with butter and remaining berries. Garnish with whipped cream and whole berries. Serves 8. Strawberries, peaches, raspberries, or boysenberries make delicious shortcakes.

Cranberry Shortcake

INGREDIENTS

2 cups flour
1 cup milk or water
4 tsp. baking powder
1 tsp. salt
2½ tbs. shortening
1 to 2 tbs. melted butter
Ten-Minute Cranberry Sauce

TEN-MINUTE CRANBERRY SAUCE
1 lb. or quart
(4 cups) cranberries
2 cups water
1½ to 2 cups sugar

DIRECTIONS

Preheat oven to 450°F

METHOD Sift flour, salt and baking powder together; cut in shortening with knife; add liquid. Roll on slightly floured board; cut to make two layers for cake pans or individual portions. Place one layer in pan, spread with melted butter; cover with other layer and bake in hot oven 15 to 20 minutes. Separate. While hot, place Ten-Minute Cranberry Sauce between and on top. Serve hot with either plain or whipped cream.

TEN-MINUTE CRANBERRY SAUCE (Stewed Cranberries)
METHOD Boil sugar and water together 5 minutes/add cranberries and boil without stirring (5 minutes is usually sufficient) until all the skins pop open. Remove from the fire when the popping stops, and allow the sauce to remain in vessel undisturbed until cool.

Wonder Chocolate Layer Cake

DIRECTIONS

Preheat oven to 375°F

Sift flour once, measure, add baking powder and salt, and sift together. Cream butter thoroughly, add sugar gradually, and cream together well. Add egg and beat very thoroughly. Add flour, alternately with milk, a small amount at a time, beating after each addition until smooth. Add vanilla. Bake in two greased 8-inch layer pans in moderate oven (375°F.) 25 minutes. Cool thoroughly. Spread Chocolate Wonder Frosting between layers and on top of cake.

CHOCOLATE WONDER FROSTING

Soften cream cheese with milk. Add sugar, 1 cup at a time, blending after each addition. Add chocolate and salt and beat until smooth. Makes enough frosting to cover two 8-inch layers.

INGREDIENTS

2 cups sifted cake flour
1 cup sugar
2 tsp. baking powder
1 egg, unbeaten
¼ tsp. salt
¾ cup milk
4 tbs. butter or shortening
1 tsp. vanilla extract

CHOCOLATE WONDER FROSTING

3 oz. cream cheese
2 squares (2 oz.) unsweetened chocolate, melted & cooled
2 to 3 tbs. milk
2 cups sifted confectioners' sugar
Dash of salt

Magazine advertisement, 1927

Chocolate Layer or Loaf Cake

INGREDIENTS

2 cups sifted cake flour
2 tsp. baking powder
¼ tsp. salt
l/3 cup butter or shortening
1 cup sugar
1 egg, unbeaten
¾ cup milk
1 tsp. vanilla extract

MELLOW CHOCOLATE FROSTING
3 cups sifted
confectioners' sugar
3 tbs. melted butter
1 tsp. vanilla extract
⅛ tsp. salt
4½ squares unsweetened
chocolate, melted & cooled
½ cup milk

DIRECTIONS

Preheat oven to 375°F

Sift flour once, measure, add baking powder and salt, and sift together.
Cream butter, add sugar gradually, and cream together until light and fluffy. Add egg and beat very thoroughly. Add flour, alternately with milk, a small amount at a time, beating after each addition until smooth. Add vanilla. Bake in two greased 8-inch layer pans in moderate oven (375°F.) 20 to 25 minutes. Or bake in greased pan, 8 x 8 x 2 inches, in moderate oven (350°F.) 45 to 50 minutes. Cool thoroughly. Spread with Mellow Chocolate Frosting and chopped nuts.

MELLOW CHOCOLATE FROSTING
Combine ingredients in order in deep bowl, beating with rotary beater until blended. Place bowl in pan of cracked ice or ice water and continue beating until just thick enough to spread. Remove from ice water (frosting will continue to thicken). If necessary, add 1 to 2 tbs. additional milk or cream until of right consistency to spread. Makes enough frosting to cover tops and sides of two 8- or 9-inch layers, or top and Sides of 8 x 8 x 2-inch cake (generously).

Devil's Food Cake

DIRECTIONS

Preheat oven to 350°F
Sift flour once, measure, add soda, and sift together. Cream butter thoroughly and add butter gradually and cream together until light and fluffy. Add eggs, one at a time, beating well after each; then add chocolate and blend. Add flour, alternately with milk, a small amount at a time, beating after each addition until smooth. Add vanilla. Bake in three greased 8-inch layer pans in moderate oven (350°F.) 30 minutes. Cool thoroughly. Spread Seven Minute Frosting between layers and on top and sides of cake.

SEVEN MINUTE FROSTING
Combine egg whites, sugar, water, and corn syrup in top of double boiler, beating until thoroughly mixed. Place over rapidly boiling water, beat constantly and cook 7 minutes, or until frosting will stand in peaks. Remove from boiling water; add vanilla and beat until thick enough to spread.

MARSHMALLOW FROSTING Add 1 cup marshmallows, quartered, to Seven Minute Frosting, folding them lightly into frosting just before it is put on cake.

ORANGE SEVEN MINUTE FROSTING Omit corn syrup and substitute 3 tablespoons orange juice for 3 tablespoons water in recipe for Seven Minute Frosting. Flavor with ½ tsp. grated orange rind and 2 drops almond extract instead of vanilla.

PEPPERMINT FROSTING Use recipe for Seven Minute Frosting. Color a delicate shell-pink by adding a very small amount of red coloring, and flavor to taste with oil of peppermint (only a few drops are necessary).

INGREDIENTS

2 cups sifted cake flour
1 tsp. soda
½ cup butter or shortening
1¼ cups brown sugar, firmly packed
2 eggs or 3 egg yolks, unbeaten
3 squares (3 oz.) unsweetened chocolate, melted
1 cup milk
1 tsp. vanilla extract

7 MINUTE FROSTING
2 egg whites, unbeaten
1½ cups sugar
5 tbs. water
1½ tsp. light corn syrup
1 tsp. vanilla extract

Favorite Devil's Food Cake

INGREDIENTS

2 cups sifted cake flour
2 eggs unbeaten
6 squares (6 oz.)
  unsweetened chocolate,
  melted & cooled
1 tsp. soda
½ cup butter or shortening
1¼ cups milk
1¼ cups brown sugar,
firmly packed
1 tsp. vanilla extract

DIVINITY FROSTING

3 cups sugar
1⅓ cups boiling water
1 tsp. light corn syrup
4 egg whites, stiffly beaten
1 tsp. vanilla extract

DIRECTIONS

Preheat oven to 350°F

Sift flour once, measure, add soda, and sift together. Cream butter thoroughly, add sugar gradually, and cream together until light and fluffy. Add eggs, one at a time, and beat well. Add chocolate and beat well. Add flour, alternately with milk, a small amount at a time. Beat after each addition until smooth. Add vanilla. Bake in three 9-inch layer pans in moderate oven (325°F.) 30 minutes. Spread with Divinity Frosting.

DIVINITY FROSTING

Combine sugar, corn syrup, and water. Place over low flame and stir constantly until sugar is dissolved and mixture boils. Continue cooking until a small amount of syrup forms a soft ball in cold water, or spins a long thread when dropped from tip of spoon (140°F.). Pour syrup in fine stream over egg whites, beating constantly. Add vanilla. Continue beating until stiff enough to spread on cake. Makes enough frosting to cover tops and sides of three 9-inch layers.

Chocolate Fudge Cake

INGREDIENTS

2 cups sifted cake flour
2 tsp. baking powder
½ tsp. soda
¼ tsp. salt
½ cup butter or shortening
1 cup sugar
2 egg yolks, well beaten
3 squares (3 oz.) unsweetened chocolate, melted & cooled
1¼ cups milk
1 tsp. vanilla extract
2 egg whites, stiffly beaten

FUDGE FROSTING

2 squares (2 oz.) unsweetened chocolate, cut in pieces
Dash of salt
2 tbs. light corn syrup
⅔ cup cold milk
2 tbs. butter
2 cups sugar
1 tsp. vanilla extract

DIRECTIONS

Preheat oven to 350°F

Sift flour once, measure, add baking powder, soda, and salt, and sift together. Cream butter thoroughly, add sugar gradually, and cream together until light and fluffy. Add egg yolks and chocolate; then add flour, alternately with milk, a small amount at a time. Beat after each addition until smooth. Add vanilla. Fold in egg whites. Bake in greased loaf pans in moderate oven (350°F.) 30 minutes. Cover top and sides of cake with Fudge Frosting.

FUDGE FROSTING

Add chocolate to milk and place over low flame. Cook until mixture is smooth and blended, stirring constantly. Add sugar, salt, and corn syrup, and stir until sugar is dissolved and mixture boils. Continue cooking, without stirring, until a small amount of mixture forms a very soft ball in cold water (232°F.). Remove from fire. Add butter and vanilla. Cool to lukewarm (110°F.). Beat until of right consistency to spread.

Magazine advertisement, 1930

Everyday Chocolate Layer Cake

QUICK CHOCOLATE FROSTING

4 tbs. butter
4 squares (4 oz.) unsweetened chocolate, melted & cooled
1/3 cup hot milk
3 cups sifted confectioners' sugar
1 tsp. vanilla extract
1/8 tsp. salt

INGREDIENTS

2 cups sifted flour
2 tsp. baking powder
1/2 tsp. soda
1/2 tsp. salt
2/3 cup butter
1 1/4 cup sugar
1 tsp. vanilla extract
2 eggs
3 squares (3 oz.) unsweetened chocolate, melted & cooled
1 cup milk

DIRECTIONS

Preheat oven to 350°F

Sift flour once, then measure and mix with baking powder soda and salt. Cream shortening until softened; add sugar gradually, beating thoroughly after each addition. Beat in vanilla, then eggs, one at a time beating until light and fluffy after each. Add melted chocolate and stir until blended. Add flour mixture alternately with milk, beating until smooth after each addition. Turn into 2 greased 8 or 9-inch layer cake pans. Bake in moderate (350 degrees F.) for 25 to 30 minutes.

QUICK CHOCOLATE FROSTING

Melt butter and chocolate in double boiler; stir until blended. Stir hot milk into sugar, and beat until smooth. Stir in vanilla, salt and chocolate mixture. Beat until smooth and thickened, about 5 minutes.

Four Square Chocolate Cake

INGREDIENTS

½ cup butter or shortening
1 tsp. salt
1 tsp. vanilla extract
1 cup sugar
2 eggs, unbeaten
2 oz. chocolate, melted & cooled
2 tsp. baking powder
¼ tsp. soda
1¾ cups sifted flour
¾ cup milk

CREAMY VANILLA FROSTING
2 tbs. butter
2 cups sifted confectioners' sugar
¾ tsp. vanilla extract
3 tbs. scalded cream
¼ tsp. salt

DIRECTIONS

Preheat oven to 350°F

Blend shortening, salt, and vanilla. Add sugar gradually and cream well. Add eggs, singly, beating well after each addition. Add chocolate and blend. Sift baking powder and soda with flour. Add flour to creamed mixture, alternately with milk, mixing after each addition until smooth. Bake in two coated 8-inch layer pans in moderate oven (350°F.) 30 to 35 minutes. Cool thoroughly. Frost each corner differently: ¼ plain, ¼ decorated with nuts, ¼ mixed with 1 oz. melted chocolate, ¼ mixed with 1 tsp. orange rind.

CREAMY VANILLA FROSTING
Combine butter, vanilla, and salt and blend. Beat in ½ cup sugar. Add hot cream, alternately with remaining sugar, beating well after each addition. Add only enough cream to make a nice spreading consistency.

Bittersweet Nougat Cake

INGREDIENTS

¾ cup cocoa
⅓ cup sugar
1¼ cups scalded milk
⅔ cup butter or shortening
1 tsp. salt
1 tsp. vanilla extract
1 cup sugar
3 eggs, unbeaten
1¼ tsp. soda
2 cups sifted flour

CHOCOLATE DRIZZLE
1 oz. semisweet chocolate
1 tsp. shortening

NOUGAT FROSTING
2 egg whites, unbeaten
1½ cups sugar
4 tbs. water
2 tbs. light corn syrup
2 tbs. honey
½ tsp. vanilla extract
¼ tsp. cream of tartar

DIRECTIONS

Preheat oven to 350°F

Mix and sift cocoa with ⅓ cup sugar. Add scalded milk gradually and stir until smooth. Cool. Blend shortening, salt, and vanilla. Add 1 cup sugar gradually and cream well. Add eggs, singly, beating well after each addition. Sift soda with flour, add flour to creamed mixture, alternately with cocoa mixture, mixing after each addition until smooth. Bake in two deep 9-inch greased layer pans in moderate oven (350°F.) 25 to 30 minutes. Cool thoroughly. Frost with Nougat Frosting as directed.

NOUGAT FROSTING
Combine egg whites, sugar, water, and corn syrup in top of double boiler, beating until thoroughly mixed. Place over rapidly boiling water, beat constantly with rotary egg beater, and cook 7 minutes, or until frosting will stand in peaks. Remove from boiling water; add vanilla and beat until thick enough to spread. To ⅓ of frosting, add ¼ cup chopped blanched almonds and spread between layers. Spread plain frosting on top and sides.

CHOCOLATE DRIZZLE
Melt chocolate with shortening and pour around edge letting it drip down over sides as shown in picture.

Chocolate Layer Cake

INGREDIENTS

2 cups brown sugar, packed
½ cup butter
2 eggs, separated
2 cups flour
½ cup buttermilk
1 tsp. baking soda
½ cup hot water
½ cup ground chocolate
1 tsp. baking powder

FILLING
¼ cup butter
1 cup powdered sugar
1 cup chopped walnuts
2 tbs. cold strong coffee

ICING
2 cups powdered sugar
1 square (1 oz.)
  unsweetened chocolate
evaporated milk

DIRECTIONS

Preheat oven to 325°F

Cream together butter and sugar. Add egg yolks and 1 cup flour, then milk, into which soda has been stirred. Add water, chocolate, and remaining cup flour and baking powder. Lastly fold in stiffly beaten egg whites. Bake in moderate (325°F) oven for 40 minutes in 2 9-inch round, greased cake pans or until done. Cool thoroughly. Fill and frost.

FILLING
Cream together butter and sugar. Add coffee and walnuts.

ICING
Melt chocolate and add to sugar. Add milk slowly until proper consistency for spreading.

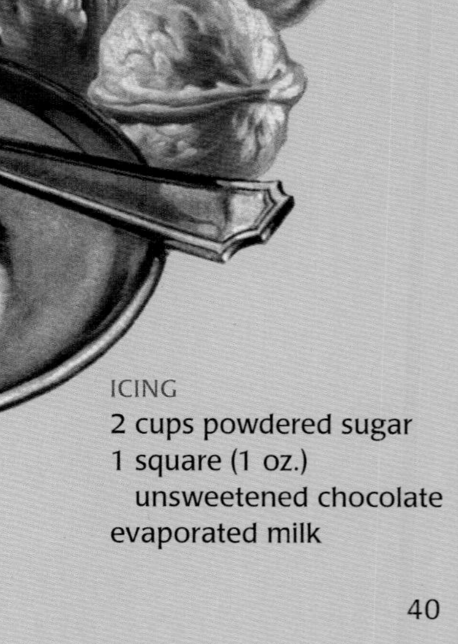

Magazine advertisement, n.d.

Chocolate Sponge

INGREDIENTS

8 oz. self-raising flour
1 tsp. baking powder
3 oz. butter
4 tbs. cocoa
Vanilla extract
½ cup sugar
1 cup hot water
2 tbs. chocolate syrup
Whipped cream for filling

CHOCOLATE GLACE ICING
2 tbs. cocoa
8 tbs confectioners′ sugar
2 tbs. water

DIRECTIONS

Preheat oven to 300°F

Sieve the flour, cocoa and sugar together. Dissolve the syrup in the water. Melt the butter and mix all the ingredients together, including the essence, but do not beat the mixture, which should be very soft. Divide the mixture evenly into two greased, 8-inch cake tins and bake in a moderately hot oven (300°F.) for 20 minutes. Cool.

When cool use whipped cream filling between the two layers. Cover with Chocolate Glace Icing.

CHOCOLATE GLACE ICING
Sieve sugar and cocoa together in a basin, then add warm water while stirring. Place basin in a receptacle of hot water until icing will coat the back of a spoon.

Chocolate Peppermint Cake

INGREDIENTS

¼ cup butter
1½ cups flour
½ tsp. salt
1 cup sugar
1 tsp. soda
2 egg yolks
1 cup buttermilk
2 squares (2 oz.)
unsweetened chocolate
1 tsp. vanilla extract

DIRECTIONS

Preheat oven to 350°F

Cream butter and sugar, add egg yolks; beat briskly. Add chocolate, melted. Sift flour, salt and soda. Add to mixture alternately with the buttermilk. Mix thoroughly. Add vanilla. Pour into 8″ square cake pan, rubbed with shortening. Bake in moderate oven (350°F.) 50 to 60 minutes. Cool.

EASY FROSTING

Put 1½ cups granulated sugar, 2 unbeaten egg whites and ⅓ cup water to cook over boiling water. Beat constantly for 4 minutes. Then add either ½ teaspoon peppermint flavoring or ¼ cup crushed peppermint candy (after-dinner mints or patties). Continue beating until frosting is thick. Remove from boiling water. Continue beating until frosting is a spreading consistency. Spread over top and sides of cake. Melt 2 squares of bittersweet chocolate. Blend with 1 teaspoon shortening. Pour and spread over top of cake, letting chocolate run down sides.

Magazine advertisement, n.d.

Sour Cream Devil's Food Cake

WITH PEPPERMINT FROSTING

INGREDIENTS

2 cups sifted cake flour
1 tsp. soda
½ tsp. salt
⅓ cup butter or shortening
1¼ cups sugar
1 egg, unbeaten
3 squares (3 oz.) unsweetened chocolate, melted & cooled
½ cup thick sour cream
¾ cup sweet milk
1 tsp. vanilla extract
Chocolate for decoration

PEPPERMINT FROSTING

2 egg whites, unbeaten
1½ cups sugar
1 tsp. vanilla extract
5 tbs. water
1½ tsp. light corn syrup
Peppermint flavoring
Red food coloring

DIRECTIONS

Preheat oven to 350°F

Sift flour once, measure, add soda and salt, and sift three together. Cream butter thoroughly, add sugar gradually, and cream well. Beat in egg, then chocolate. Add about ¼ of flour and beat well; then sour cream. Add remaining flour, alternately with milk, in small amounts, beating after each addition. Add vanilla. Bake in two greased 9-inch layer pans in moderate oven (350°F.) 30 minutes. Cool thoroughly. Spread with Sour Cream Devil's Food Cake with Peppermint Frosting. When cold but soft, sprinkle border of chocolate flakes around top.
For flakes, scrape unsweetened chocolate with sharp knife, scraping down.

PEPPERMINT FROSTING

Combine egg whites, sugar, water, and corn syrup in top of double boiler, beating until thoroughly mixed. Place over rapidly boiling water, beat constantly and cook 7 minutes, or until frosting will stand in peaks. Remove from boiling water; add vanilla and beat until thick enough to spread. Color a delicate shell pink by adding a very small amount of red coloring, and flavor to taste with oil of peppermint (only a few drops are necessary).

Ambassador Coconut Cake

INGREDIENTS

2 cups sifted cake flour
1 tsp. soda
½ tsp. salt
1 cup butter or shortening
1⅓ cups brown sugar, firmly packed
3 eggs, well beaten
4 squares (4 oz.) unsweetened chocolate, melted & cooled
⅔ cup cold water

COCONUT MOROCCO FROSTING
1 square unsweetened chocolate, melted & cooled
2 egg whites, unbeaten
1½ cups brown sugar
Dash of salt
5 tbs. water
1 tsp. vanilla extract
1 package coconut

DIRECTIONS

Preheat oven to 350°F

Sift flour once, measure, add soda and salt, and sift together. Cream butter thoroughly, add sugar gradually, and cream together until light and fluffy. Add eggs and beat well; then chocolate and blend. Add flour, alternately with water, a small amount at a time, beating after each addition until smooth. Bake in two greased deep 9-inch layer pans in moderate oven (350°F.) 30 minutes, or until done. Cool thoroughly. Spread coconut Morocco Frosting between layers and on top and sides of cake, sprinkling with coconut.

COCONUT MOROCCO FROSTING
Combine egg whites, sugar, salt, and water in top of double boiler, until thoroughly mixed. Place over rapidly boiling water, beat constantly, cook 7 minutes, or until frosting will stand in peaks. Remove from boiling water; fold in chocolate and vanilla. Spread on cake, sprinkling with coconut while frosting is soft.

Mallo-Nut Fudge Cake

INGREDIENTS

3 oz. chocolate, cut very fine
¾ cup boiling water
1¾ cups sifted cake flour
1½ cups sugar
¾ tsp. salt
½ tsp. baking powder
¾ tsp. soda
½ cup butter or shortening
½ cup buttermilk
1 tsp. vanilla extract
2 eggs, unbeaten
18 marshmallows, cut in half
½ cup chopped nuts

MINUTE-BOIL FUDGE FROSTING
2 oz. chocolate finely cut
4 tbs. butter
1½ cups sugar
1 tbs. corn syrup
7 tbs. milk
¼ tsp. salt
1 tsp. vanilla extract
5 tbs. water
1 tsp. vanilla extract

DIRECTIONS

Preheat oven to 350°F

Put chocolate in mixing bowl. Pour boiling water over chocolate and stir until melted. Cool. Sift flour, sugar, salt, baking powder, and soda into chocolate mixture. Drop in butter. Beat 2 minutes on mixer at low speed. Scrape bowl and spoon. Add buttermilk, vanilla, and eggs and beat 2 minutes on mixer at low speed. Bake in two square 8 x 8 x 2-inch coated pans in moderate oven (350°F.) 30-40 minutes. While cake is warm, press marshmallows on one layer, turned bottom-side up. Spread with Minute-Boil Fudge Frosting; put other layer on top. Add nuts to remaining frosting, spread on top of cake. Decorate each corner with a quartered marshmallow.

MINUTE-BOIL FUDGE FROSTING
Place chocolate, sugar, milk, butter, corn syrup, and salt in saucepan. Bring slowly to a full rolling boil, stirring constantly, and boil briskly 1 full minute. Cool to lukewarm. Add vanilla and beat until thick enough to spread.

A Little Book of Favorite Recipes, 1933

Velvet Fudge Cake

WITH MOCHA BUTTER CREAM FROSTING

MOCHA BUTTER CREAM FROSTING

3½ cups sifted confectioners' sugar
¼ cup cocoa
⅛ tsp. salt
½ cup butter
6 tbs. cold coffee (approx.)
½ tsp. vanilla extract

INGREDIENTS

4 squares (ozs.) unsweetened chocolate
½ cup hot water
½ cup sugar
2 cups sifted cake flour
1 tsp. soda
1 tsp. salt
½ cup shortening (at room temp.)
1 cups sugar
3 eggs, unbeaten
Milk*
1 tsp. vanilla extract

*With vegetable shortening, use ¾ cup milk. With butter or margarine, use ⅔ cup

DIRECTIONS

Use two round 9-inch layer pans, 1½ inches deep; line pans on bottoms with paper. Start oven for moderate heat (350°F.). Sift flour before measuring.

Heat chocolate with hot water in top of double boiler or bowl. Cook and stir over boiling water until chocolate is melted and mixture is thickened. Add ½ cup sugar and cook and stir 2 minutes longer. Cool to lukewarm while mixing cake. Measure sifted flour, add soda and salt, and sift together. Cream shortening, add 1¼ cups sugar gradually, and cream together until light and fluffy. Add eggs, one at a time, beating thoroughly after each. Then add flour, alternately with milk, in small amounts, beating after each addition until smooth. Add chocolate mixture and vanilla; blend. Pour batter into pans. Bake in moderate oven (350°F.) about 30 minutes. Cool thoroughly. Frost with Mocha Butter Cream Frosting.

MOCHA BUTTER CREAM FROSTING

Sift together sugar, cocoa, and salt. Cream shortening. Add part of sugar mixture gradually, blending after each addition until light and fluffy. Add the remaining sugar, alternately with coffee, until of spreading consistency, beating after each addition until smooth. Add vanilla; blend.

Black Eyed Susan Cake

INGREDIENTS

4 squares (4 oz.) unsweetened chocolate
½ cup hot water
1¾ cup sugar
2 cups sifted cake flour
1 tsp. soda
1 tsp. salt
½ cup butter or shortening
1¼ cups sugar
3 eggs, unbeaten
⅔ cup Milk
1 tsp. vanilla extract

DIRECTIONS

Line bottoms of pans with paper; grease.
Use two round 9-inch layer pans, 1½ inches deep. Start oven for moderate heat (350°F.). Sift flour once before measuring. (All measurements are level.)
1. Combine chocolate and water in top of double boiler. Cook and stir over boiling water until chocolate is melted and mixture thickens. Add ½ cup sugar and cook and stir 2 minutes. Remove from heat. Cool to lukewarm.
2. Sift flour once, measure, add soda and salt, and sift together.
3. Cream shortening, add 1¼ cups sugar gradually, and cream together until light and fluffy. Add eggs, one at a time, beating thoroughly after each. Add ½ of the flour and beat until smooth. Add milk and remaining flour, alternately, in small amounts, beating after each addition until smooth. Then add vanilla and chocolate mixture and blend.
Turn batter into pans and bake in moderate oven (350°F.) 30 to 35 minutes, or until done. Cool cake in pans on cake racks for 5 minutes. Then loosen from sides with spatula. Turn out, remove the paper, and turn right-side up on racks to cool before frosting.
Spread Golden Orange Frosting between layers and on top and sides. Decorate top of cake with black-eyed Susan design, using thinly sliced orange rind for petals and semi-sweet chocolate chips for centers of flowers.

GOLDEN ORANGE FROSTING

Cream together ⅓ cup butter, 1½ tablespoons grated orange rind, 1 teaspoon grated lemon rind, and ¼ teaspoon salt. Add 1 unbeaten egg yolk and mix well. Then add 3½ cups sifted confectioners' sugar, alternately with 1 tablespoon orange juice and 2 teaspoons lemon juice, beating well after each addition.

Brownie Nut Cake

DIRECTIONS

Sift together
2½ cups sifted flour
2½ cups sugar
4 tsp. double-action baking powder
1 tsp. salt
12 tbsp. cocoa
⅔ cup butter
1 cup milk

Beat 2 minutes.

Add 4 eggs
½ cup more milk

Beat 2 minutes.

Fold in 1 cup chopped nuts

PAN SIZE: square, 9 x 9 x 2-in.

TEMPERATURE: 350° (moderate oven).

TIME: 30 to 35 minutes.

Frost with Butterscotch Icing.

BUTTERSCOTCH ICING
Melt 6 tbsp. butter and heat until golden brown. Remove from heat. Blend in 2 cups sifted confectioners' sugar. Add 1 tsp. vanilla. Stir in about 4 tbsp. hot water (until icing will spread smoothly). (Note: Spread thinly.) Amount: icing for 2-layer cake.

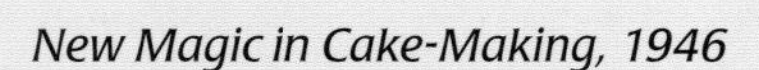

Raisin Fudge Cake

WITH ALMONDS

INGREDIENTS

½ cup butter or substitute
1½ cups brown sugar
2 egg-yolks
½ cup brown sugar
1 cup chopped raisins
4 squares (4 oz.) chocolate,
 melted & cooled
½ cup hot water
½ cup buttermilk
2½ cups cake flour
1 tsp. soda
½ tsp. cinnamon
¼ tsp. cloves
2 egg-whites
⅓ cup blanched almonds
2 tbs. granulated sugar

DIRECTIONS

Beat the butter to a cream and gradually work in the first measure of sugar (the sugar should be well pressed down in the cup). Beat the egg-yolks; beat in the second measure of sugar, the raisins, and melted chocolate. Sift together the flour, soda, and spices and add them to the first mixture alternately with the water and buttermilk; lastly, fold in the egg-whites, beaten very lightly. Turn into a tube cake pan. Split the almonds and press one edge of each half nut in the top of the cake; sift the sugar over the almonds and top of the cake. Bake about 50 minutes. Cool thoroughly.

Feather Spice Cake

FLUFFY MOCHA FROSTING

⅔ cup butter
½ tsp. salt
4 cups sifted confectioners' sugar
⅔ cup strong coffee (about)
7 tbs. breakfast cocoa
2 tsp. vanilla extract
1½ cup broken walnut meats, toasted

INGREDIENTS

4½ cups sifted cake flour
5 tsp. baking powder
½ tsp. salt
½ tsp. cloves
2 tsp. cinnamon
1 tsp. mace
1 cup butter or shortening
2 cup sugar
4 eggs, unbeaten
⅔ cup molasses
1½ cup milk

DIRECTIONS

Preheat oven to 375°F

Sift flour once, measure, add baking powder, salt, and spices, and sift together. Cream butter thoroughly, add sugar gradually, and cream together until light and fluffy. Add eggs, one at a time, beating thoroughly after each. Then add molasses and blend. Add flour, alternately with milk, a small amount at a time, beating after each addition until smooth. Bake in two greased 9-inch layer pans in moderate oven (375°F.) 25 minutes, or until done. Cool thoroughly. Spread Fluffy Mocha Frosting between layers and on top and sides of cake; sprinkle nuts on sides.

FLUFFY MOCHA FROSTING

Cream butter. Sift sugar, cocoa, and salt together. Add part of the sugar mixture gradually to butter, blending after each addition. Add remaining sugar mixture, alternately with coffee, until of right consistency to spread. Beat after each addition until smooth. Add vanilla. Spread on cake.

Coffee Cake

INGREDIENTS

2 cups flour
4 tsp. baking powder
½ tsp. salt
2 tbs. shortening
3 tbs. sugar
1 cup milk

TOP MIXTURE
3 tbs. flour
3 tbs. sugar
1 tbs. cinnamon
3 tbs. shortening

DIRECTIONS

Preheat oven to 400°F

Mix and sift dry ingredients; add melted shortening and enough milk to make very stiff batter. Mix well and spread in greased pan; add top mixture. Bake about thirty minutes in moderate oven at 400°F.

TOP MIXTURE
Mix dry ingredients; rub in shortening and spread thickly over top of dough before baking.

From Anyone Can Bake, 1927

Banana Spice Cake

INGREDIENTS

2¼ cups sifted cake flour
1¼ cups sugar
2½ tsp. baking powder
½ tsp. baking soda
½ tsp. salt
⅛ tsp. cloves
1¼ tsp. cinnamon
½ tsp. nutmeg
½ cup shortening or butter
1½ cups mashed ripe bananas
2 eggs
1 tsp. vanilla extract
Banana & nuts to decorate

7 MINUTE FROSTING
2 egg whites, unbeaten
1½ cups sugar
5 tbs. water
1½ tsp. light corn syrup
1 tsp. vanilla extract

DIRECTIONS

Preheat oven to 375°F

Set the oven for moderately hot, 375°F. Grease and flour two 8-inch round cake pans.

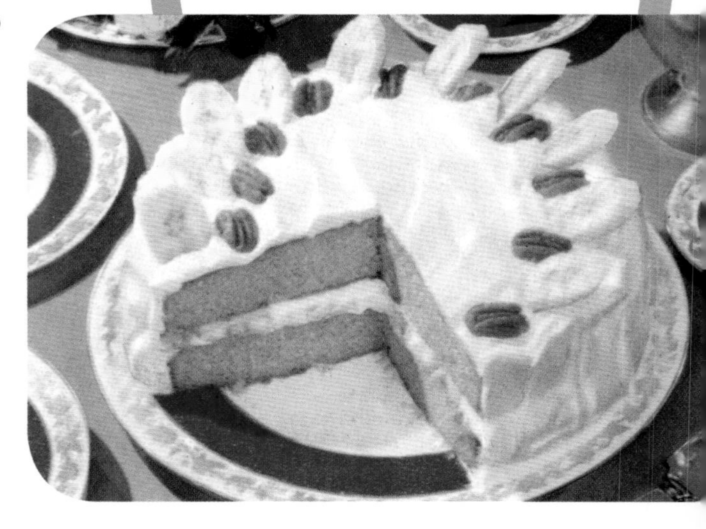

Sift together first 8 ingredients into a large mixing bowl. Add shortening, ½ cup of the bananas, and eggs. Beat 2 minutes by hand or on an electric mixer at slow to medium speed. Scrape down bowl and spoon or beater frequently during mixing. Add remaining 1 cup bananas and vanilla. Beat 1 minute longer, scraping down bowl and spoon or beater frequently. Turn into pans. Bake 25 minutes or until cake springs back when lightly touched with fingertip. Cool in pans 5 minutes. Remove from pan and cool on a rack. Frost with Seven Minute Frosting. Decorate with banana slices and whole walnut or pecan meats.

SEVEN MINUTE FROSTING
Combine egg whites, sugar, water, and corn syrup in top of double boiler, beating until thoroughly mixed. Place over rapidly boiling water, beat constantly with rotary egg beater, and cook 7 minutes, or until frosting will stand in peaks. Remove from boiling water; add vanilla and beat until thick enough to spread.

Apple Sauce Cake

INGREDIENTS

1¾ cups sifted flour
½ tsp. salt
1½ tsp. cinnamon
1 tsp. allspice
1 tsp. nutmeg
¼ tsp. cloves
1 tsp. baking soda
½ cup butter or shortening
1 cup sugar
1 egg, well beaten
1 cup unsweetened apple sauce

DIRECTIONS

Set oven for moderate, 350°F. Grease and flour a loaf pan, 9 x 5 x 3 inches.

Sift together first 7 ingredients. Cream shortening. Add sugar gradually; continue beating until light and fluffy. Add egg and beat well. Stir in apple sauce. Add sifted dry ingredients; stir only enough to blend. Pour into pan. Bake 50-60 minutes or until cake springs back when lightly touched with fingertip. Cool in pan 5 minutes. Remove from pan and cool on a rack. Frost with Butter Frosting.

BUTTER FROSTING

Blend together 2 cups sifted confectioners' sugar, and¼ cup butter or margarine. Gradually add about 2 tablespoons cream. Stir until smooth. Add ½ tsp. vanilla, ½ tsp. orange extract, and a few drops each yellow and red food coloring.

Arabian Ribbon Cake

RAISIN ORANGE FILLING
3 tbs. cake flour
½ cup sugar
1 tbs. grated orange rind
½ cup orange juice
¾ cup water
2 cups raisins, finely chopped
⅔ cup nuts, chopped & toasted

DIRECTIONS

Preheat oven to 375°F
Sift flour once, measure, add baking powder and salt, and sift together. Cream butter, add sugar gradually, and cream together until light and fluffy. Add egg yolks, one at a time, beating thoroughly after each. Add flour, alternately with milk, a small amount at a time, beating after each addition until smooth. Add vanilla. Beat egg whites until they will hold up in moist peaks. Stir quickly but thoroughly into batter.
Fill one greased 9-inch layer pan with one-third of mixture. To remaining mixture, add spices and molasses and blend. Turn into two greased 9-inch layer pans. Bake layers in moderate oven (375°F.) 20 to 25 minutes. Arrange white layer between spice layers. Spread Raisin Orange Filling between layers and Tart Lemon Frosting on top and sides of cake. Sprinkle with grated lemon rind.

TART LEMON FROSTING
Add lemon rind to butter; cream well. Add part of sugar gradually, blending after each addition. Add remaining sugar, alternately with lemon juice, until of right consistency to spread. Beat thoroughly after each addition. Add salt.

RAISIN ORANGE FILLING
Combine flour, sugar, and orange rind; add orange juice, water, and raisins and cook gently 5 minutes, or until thickened, stirring constantly. Add nuts and cool to lukewarm. Makes enough filling to spread between three 9-inch layers.

INGREDIENTS

3 cups sifted cake flour
3 tsp. baking powder
½ tsp. salt
⅔ cup butter or shortening
1½ cups sugar
3 egg yolks, unbeaten
1¼ cups milk
1 tsp. vanilla extract
3 egg whites
1½ tsp. cinnamon
¼ tsp. cloves
½ tsp. mace
½ tsp. nutmeg
3 tbs. dark molasses

TART LEMON FROSTING
3 cups sifted confectioners' sugar
1 tsp. grated lemon rind
4 tbs. butter
3 tbs. lemon juice
Dash of salt

Cake Secrets, 1941

Tropical Spice Cake

INGREDIENTS

4½ cups sifted cake flour
½ tsp. cloves
5 tsp. baking powder
1 cup butter or shortening
½ tsp. salt
2 cups sugar
2 tsp. cinnamon
4 eggs, unbeaten
1 tsp. mace
⅔ cup molasses
1½ cups milk

TROPICAL FROSTING
2 egg whites, unbeaten
1 cup sugar
1 tbs. water
3 tbs. lemon juice
½ tsp grated lemon rind
2 drops almond extract

DIRECTIONS

Preheat oven to 375°F
Sift flour once, measure, add baking powder, salt, and spices, and sift together. Cream butter thoroughly, add sugar gradually, and cream together until light and fluffy. Add eggs, one at a time, beating thoroughly after each. Then add molasses and blend. Add flour, alternately with milk, a small amount at a time, beating after each addition until smooth. Bake in two greased 9-inch layer pans in moderate oven (375°F.) 25 minutes, or until done. Cool thoroughly.

TROPICAL FROSTING
Combine egg whites, sugar, water, and lemon juice. Cook as for Seven Minute Frosting (see page 52). Add lemon rind and almond extract and beat until thick enough to spread. To 1/3 of frosting, add ½ cup cut raisins and ½ package shredded coconut. Spread between layers of cake. Cover top and sides with remaining frosting and sprinkle with remaining ½ package of coconut.

White Fruit Cake

INGREDIENTS

4 cups sifted cake flour
1 tsp. baking powder
½ tsp. soda
½ tsp. salt
1 cup butter or shortening
1½ cups sugar
1 tbs. lemon juice
1 lb. Sultana raisins
½ lb. citron, cut fine
½ lb. each crystallized ginger,
orange & lemon peel,
pineapple & red cherries,
cut fine
1 lb blanched almonds, chopped
10 egg whites, beaten stiff

DIRECTIONS

Preheat oven to 250°F
Sift flour once, measure, add baking powder, soda, and salt, and sift together three times. Sift 1 cup of this flour mixture over fruits and nuts; mix thoroughly. Cream shortening until light and fluffy, add sugar gradually, and cream thoroughly. Add remaining flour mixture to creamed mixture, a small amount at a time. Beat after each addition until smooth. Add lemon juice, fruits, and nuts. Fold in egg whites. Pour in greased tube pan prepared with a paper lining in the bottom. Bake in slow oven (250°F.) 2½ hours, then increase to 300°F. for 15 minutes. Makes 6 pounds.

Magazine advertisement, 1927

INGREDIENTS

1½ cups sugar
¾ cup butter
1 cup milk
3 cups pastry flour
4 tsp. baking powder
½ tsp. salt
4 egg whites
1 tsp. lemon extract
1½ cups dried figs,
    finely chopped & floured
1 tbs. molasses
1 tsp. cinnamon
1 tsp. nutmeg

DIRECTIONS

Cream sugar and butter: add milk. Sift flour, salt, and baking powder. Add one-half of the flour, then well beaten egg whites, then rest of flour and extract.

Take two-thirds of the mixture and add figs, molasses, cinnamon and nutmeg.

Put in a greased and lightly floured round tube pan a spoonful of light mixture and then a spoonful of dark mixture alternately as for marble cake. Bake in moderate oven at 350°. Bake about 55 minutes.

From Anyone Can Bake, 1927

Angel Food Cake

INGREDIENTS

1 cup cake flour
1 tsp. cream of tartar
1⅓ cups sugar
½ tsp. vanilla extract
½ tsp. almond extract
11 egg whites (1⅓ cups)
¼ tsp. salt

DIRECTIONS

Preheat oven to 325°F

Sift flour once before measuring. After measuring sift with sugar. Beat egg whites with wire whip until "foamy", add salt, beat for few seconds and add cream of tartar. Continue beating "rapidly" until egg whites will stand up in peaks when whip is drawn up through them. Pour the sugar lightly into the egg mixture and fold in carefully. Add the flour and fold in gently until mixture is smooth. Fold in flavoring last.

Bake in un-greased Angel Food pan for 60 minutes, as follows: First 20 minutes at 325°F., then 40 minutes at 300°F. (slow oven). When baked, remove from oven and invert pan for 1 hour before removing.

Sunshine Cake

INGREDIENTS

1 cup sifted cake flour
½ tsp. cream of tartar
1 cup sifted sugar
4 egg yolks beaten until thick and lemon-colored
¼ tsp. salt
6 egg whites
½ tsp. lemon extract

DIRECTIONS

Preheat oven to 300°F

Sift flour once, measure, add ½ of sugar, and sift together. Add salt to egg whites and beat with wire whisk. When foamy, add cream of tartar, and continue beating until whisk leaves faint line when drawn across surface of egg whites. Add remaining sugar gradually, and continue beating as before, until texture is very fine and egg whites are stiff enough to hold up in peaks, but not dry. Fold in egg yolks and lemon extract. Sift small amount of flour over mixture and fold in carefully; continue until all is used. Pour into un-greased tube pan and bake in slow oven (300°F.) 30 minutes, then increase heat slightly (325°F.) and bake 35 minutes longer. Remove from oven and invert pan 1 hour, or until cake is thoroughly cold.

Sprinkle lightly with powdered sugar, if desired; but do not frost. Serve in wedges to accompany ice cream, jellied desserts, or fruits. This cake will keep moist and fresh for several days if stored carefully in a cake safe or other suitable container. It is a fine, delicate sponge cake, especially suited to summer entertaining.

The Latest Cake Secrets, 1934

Angel Food Cake

WITH STRAWBERRY ICING

INGREDIENTS

1 cup sifted cake flour
1½ cups sifted granulated sugar
10 egg whites (1¼ cups)
¼ tsp. salt
1¼ tsp. cream of tartar
1 tsp. vanilla extract
¼ tsp. almond extract

STRAWBERRY ICING

3 cups sifted confectioners' sugar
Dash of salt
2 tsp. lemon juice
¼ cup crushed or sieved fresh strawberries

DIRECTIONS

Preheat oven to 325°F

Sift flour once, measure, add ½ cup sugar, and sift together four times. Beat egg whites and salt with rotary egg beater or flat wire whisk. When foamy, add cream of tartar and continue beating until eggs are stiff enough to hold up in peaks, but not dry. Add remaining sugar, 2 tablespoons at a time, beating with rotary egg beater or whisk after each addition until sugar is just blended. Fold in flavoring. Then sift about ¼ cup flour over mixture and fold in lightly; repeat until all is used. Turn into un-greased 10-inch angel food pan.
Cut gently through batter with knife to remove bubbles. Bake in slow oven (325°F.) about 1 hour. Remove from oven; invert 1 hour to cool. Spread Strawberry Icing thinly on top and sides of cake.

STRAWBERRY ICING

Add 3 cups sugar, salt, and lemon juice to the crushed fruit, mixing well. Makes enough icing to cover top and sides of angel food cake.

Strawberry Festival Cake

INGREDIENTS

¾ cup butter, or shortening
1½ tsp. almond extract
½ tsp. vanilla extract
1 tsp. salt
2 cups sugar
3 tsp. baking powder
6 egg whites, stiffly beaten
3¼ cups sifted flour
½ cup milk
½ cup water

FRESH STRAWBERRY ICING
4 tbs. butter
4 cups sifted confectioners' sugar
1 tsp. lemon juice
⅓ cup crushed berries
¼ tsp. salt (about)

DIRECTIONS

Preheat oven to 350°F

Blend shortening, flavoring extracts, and salt. Add sugar gradually and cream well. Sift baking powder with flour. Add flour to creamed mixture, alternately with combined milk and water, mixing after each addition until smooth. Fold in egg whites. Bake in three 9-inch coated layer pans in moderate oven (350°F.) 25 to 30 minutes. Cool thoroughly. Frost with Fresh Strawberry Icing.

FRESH STRAWBERRY ICING
Combine butter, lemon juice, and salt and blend. Beat in ½ cup sugar. Add strawberries, alternately with remaining sugar, beating well after each addition.

Down-South White Cake

WITH PENUCHE FROSTING

INGREDIENTS

½ cup butter
¾ tsp. salt
1 tsp. vanilla extract
1 cup sugar
2½ tsp. baking powder
2¼ cups sifted flour
¾ cup milk
3 egg whites, stiffly beaten

PENUCHE FROSTING

¾ cup brown sugar, firmly packed
¼ cup granulated sugar
⅛ tsp. salt
⅓ cup milk
1 tbs. butter
1 tsp. cream

DIRECTIONS

Preheat oven to 350°F

Blend butter, salt and vanilla. Add sugar gradually and cream well. Sift baking powder with flour. Add flour to creamed mixture, alternately with milk, mixing after each addition until smooth. Fold in egg whites. Bake in coated 8-inch tube pan in moderate oven (350°) minutes. Frost with Penuche Frosting, decorate with walnuts.

PENUCHE FROSTING

Combine sugars, salt, milk and butter in saucepan and bring to boil, stirring constantly until sugar is dissolved. Cook slowly, keeping crystals washed down from sides of pain until mixture forms a soft ball in cold water (232°F.). Cool to lukewarm. Beat until mixture thickens slightly. Add cream and beat until thick enough to spread. Spread on top and sides of cake.

Lemon Cream Sponge Cake

INGREDIENTS

1 cup cake flour, sifted
1 cup sugar
1½ tsp. grated lemon rind
2 tbs. water
5 egg yolks
1½ tbs. lemon juice
5 egg whites
¼ tsp. salt
½ tsp. cream of tartar

LEMON CREAM FILLING

5 tbs. cake flour
1 cup sugar
1 egg
⅓ cup lemon juice
⅔ cup water
2 tbs. butter
1 tsp. grated lemon rind
½ cup cream, whipped

DIRECTIONS

Preheat oven to 325°F

Add ½ cup sugar, lemon rind and water to egg yolks and beat until very thick and light. Add lemon juice gradually, beating constantly. Add flour all at once, then stir until just blended. Beat egg whites and salt with whisk until foamy. When foamy, add cream of tartar and beat until stiff enough to hold up in peaks, but not dry. Add remaining ½ cup sugar, about 2 tablespoons at a time, beating well after each addition. Fold in egg yolk mixture. Turn into 2 ungreased 9-inch layer pans. Cut gently through batter with knife to remove air bubbles. Bake in slow oven (325°) 30 minutes, or until done. Remove from oven and invert pan 1 hour, or until cake is thoroughly cold. Spread Lemon Cream Filling between layers of cooled cake and sprinkle top with confectioners' sugar.

LEMON CREAM FILLING

Combine flour and sugar in top of double boiler; add egg, lemon juice, water and butter, mixing thoroughly. Place over boiling water and cook 10 minutes, stirring constantly. Chill. Fold in lemon rind and whipped cream. Any excess filling may be used as a sauce for cake.

Toasted Almond Angel Food

Preheat oven to 375°F

PREPARATIONS Let eggs stand at room temperature an hour or two before using. Use un-greased 10-inch tube pan. Start oven for moderate heat (375°F.). Sift flour once before measuring. Sift sugar also. (All measurements are level.)

MEASURE INTO SIFTER: 1 cup + 2 tbs sifted cake flour and ½ cup sifted granulated sugar

MEASURE INTO LARGE MIXING BOWL: 1¼ cups (10) egg whites and ¼ teaspoon salt

HAVE READY:
1¼ tsp. cream of tartar
1 tsp. vanilla extract
1 cup toasted slivered almonds
1 cup sifted granulated sugar
¼ tsp. almond extract

THE MIXING METHOD
1. Sift flour and ½ cup sugar together. 2. Beat egg whites and salt with flat wire whisk or rotary egg beater until foamy. Sprinkle in cream of tartar and continue beating until eggs are stiff enough to hold up in soft peaks, but are still moist and glossy. 3. Add remaining 1 cup sugar in 4 additions by sprinkling 4 tablespoons at a time over egg whites and beating 25 strokes or turns each time. Add flavorings and beat 10 strokes or turns. 4. Add flour-and-sugar mixture in 4 additions, sifting it over the egg whites. Fold in each addition with flat wire whisk or large spoon, turning bowl gradually. Use 15 complete fold-over strokes each time. After the last addition, use 10 to 20 additional fold-over strokes.

BAKING Turn batter into un-greased 10-inch tube pan. Bake in moderate oven (375°F.) 30 to 35 minutes, or until done.

COOLING Remove from oven, invert pan on cake rack, and let stand 1 hour, or until cake is cool. To remove cake, loosen from sides of pan with a spatula and around tube with slender knife, gently drawing cake away from pan. Spread top and sides of cake with Rich Almond Frosting. (To avoid tearing cake, first distribute frosting on top and sides in spoonfuls, then spread evenly.) Press toasted slivered almonds into the frosting on sides of the cake.

RICH ALMOND FROSTING
Cream ½ cup butter until soft. Add dash salt. Then add 1¾ cups sifted confectioners sugar gradually, a small amount at a time blending well after each addition. Add½ teaspoon almond extract, and 4 tsp. milk. Beat until frosting is of the right consistency to spread. Add more milk if necessary.

Ambrosia Chiffon Cake

INGREDIENTS

1 cup + 2 tbs sifted cake flour
1½ tsp. baking powder
¾ cup sugar
¼ cup vegetable oil
2 egg yolks, unbeaten
6 tbs. water
1 tbs. grated orange rind
½ cup coconut
½ tsp. vanilla extract
½ cup (4 to 5) egg whites
½ tsp. salt
¼ tsp. cream of tartar

AMBROSIA CREAM
2 tbs confectioners' sugar
1 cup heavy cream
1 tsp. vanilla extract
¼ tsp. almond extract

DIRECTIONS

Let the eggs stand at room temperature an hour or two before using.

Have ready un-greased 8 x 8 x 2-inch square pan. Start the oven for moderate heat (350°F.). Sift flour once before measuring.

THE MIXING METHOD Measure sifted flour into sifter, add baking powder and sugar, and set aside. Measure into mixing bowl the oil, egg yolks, water, orange rind, coconut, and vanilla.

Sift in dry ingredients. Beat ½ minute at low speed of mixer, or 75 strokes by hand. Beat egg whites, salt, and cream of tartar with egg beater or at high speed of electric beater until mixture will stand in very stiff peaks—about 3 minutes. (The egg whites should be beaten stiffer than for meringue or angel food.) Do not under beat. Fold egg yolk mixture thoroughly into egg whites with a large spoon, flat wire whisk, or rubber scraper. Do not stir or beat.

BAKING Pour batter into pan. Bake in a moderate oven (350°F.) about 30 minutes. Cool cake in pan, upside down, for 1 hour, resting corners of pan on two other pans. To remove cake, loosen from sides of pan with knife and gently pull out cake.

SERVING Split cake. Spread with Ambrosia Cream, orange sections, and coconut.

AMBROSIA CREAM
Combine ingredients in bowl. Chill thoroughly. Then beat until cream will hold its shape. Pile lightly over cake. Makes 2 cups.

Cake Secrets, n.d.

Jelly Roll

INGREDIENTS

¾ cup cake flour
¾ cup sugar
3 eggs
1 tbs. milk
¾ tsp. baking powder
1 tbs. melted butter
⅓ tsp. salt
1 tsp. vanilla extract
1 cup jelly, your choice

DIRECTIONS

Preheat oven to 400°F

Sift flour once then measure. Add salt and baking powder and sift together. Beat eggs until light and creamy. Gradually add sugar, creaming together thoroughly. Add milk and melted butter. Gradually fold in flour. Add vanilla. Bake in 10 x 15-inch pan lined with greased paper, for 12 to 14 minutes at 400°F. (hot oven). Any large flat bottom pan will serve. Fold sharp ridges in the greased paper to hold batter to proper size. When baked turn the cake bottom up, immediately onto folded cloth dusted with powdered sugar. Pull off paper. With sharp knife trim off crisp edges. Immediately spread jelly and with cloth to aid, roll carefully. Leave covered with cloth while cooling.

Delicious Cakes – Proved Recipes, n.d.

Chocolate Sponge Roll

INGREDIENTS

6 tablespoons cake flour
½ teaspoon baking powder
¼ teaspoon salt
¾ cup sifted sugar
4 egg whites, stiffly beaten
4 egg yolks, beaten until thick
1 teaspoon vanilla extract
2 squares (2 ozs.) unsweetened
chocolate, melted and cooled

SEVEN MINUTE FROSTING
2 egg whites, unbeaten
1½ cups sugar
5 tbs. water
1½ tsp. light corn syrup
1 tsp. vanilla extract

BITTERSWEET COATING
2 squares (2 oz.)
bittersweet chocolate
2 tsp. butter

DIRECTIONS

Preheat oven to 400°F
Sift flour once, measure, add baking powder and salt, and sift together. Fold sugar gradually into egg whites. Fold in egg yolks and vanilla. Fold in flour gradually. Then beat in chocolate, gently but thoroughly. Turn into 15 x 10-inch pan which has been greased, lined with paper to within ½ inch of edge, and again greased. Bake in hot oven (400°F.) 13 minutes. Quickly cut off crisp edges of cake and turn out on cloth covered with powdered sugar. Remove paper. Spread Seven Minute Frosting over cake and roll. Wrap in cloth and cool on rack. Cover with Bittersweet Coating.

SEVEN MINUTE FROSTING
Combine egg whites, sugar, water, and corn syrup in top of double boiler, beating until thoroughly mixed. Place over rapidly boiling water, beat constantly with rotary egg beater, and cook 7 minutes, or until frosting will stand in peaks. Remove from boiling water; add vanilla and beat until thick enough to spread.

BITTERSWEET COATING
Melt chocolate and butter over hot water and blend. Cool slightly and pour as coating over cakes which have been frosted, letting chocolate cover top entirely and run down on sides.

Chocolate Log

INGREDIENTS

1/3 cup cocoa
2/3 cup granulated sugar
3 tablespoons cake flour
1/2 teaspoon vanilla extract
1/4 teaspoon baking powder
2 tbs. confectioners' sugar
1/4 teaspoon salt
3 eggs, separated
1/8 teaspoon cream of tartar

FRENCH CHOCOLATE FROSTING
6 ozs. semisweet chocolate chips
2 tbs. butter
1 cup confectioner's sugar
1 tbs. milk
1/2 tsp. vanilla extract

MOCHA CREAM FILLING
1 cup heavy cream
1 tbs. instant coffee
1 tsp. vanilla

DIRECTIONS

Preheat oven to 350°F
Grease a jelly roll pan 10 x 15 x 1 inches. Line with waxed paper cut 1 inch smaller than pan; grease paper. Sift cocoa with next 3 ingredients; return to sifter. Whip egg whites with a rotary beater until foamy. Gradually sprinkle cream of tartar and 1/3 cup of the granulated sugar over the egg whites, whipping until stiff but not dry. Beat egg yolks until thick and lemon-colored; beat in remaining granulated sugar and vanilla. Gradually sift and stir dry ingredients into egg yolks. Fold in beaten egg whites. Spread batter evenly in pan. Bake 25 minutes.
Just before cake is done, dampen a tea towel very slightly. Sprinkle towel with confectioner's sugar; shake off excess. Turn out baked cake immediately on the tea towel. Peel of paper; trim off crisp edges with a sharp knife. Starting at long edge, gently but firmly roll up towel and cake. Lay with loose edge underneath; cool. When cold, unroll; immediately spread with filling and roll up. Remove towel and frost. To make frosting resemble tree bark: Draw the flat side of a spatula lengthwise down the roll, using short strokes. To make chocolate curls: Shave chocolate with a very sharp paring knife. Sprinkle over frosting. Cut Chocolate Log in crosswise slices and serve. Makes about 6 servings.

MOCHA CREAM FILLING Combine cream, instant coffee and vanilla in a bowl. (If coffee is granular, dissolve first in vanilla and a little water, if necessary.) Whip until stiff. Makes enough to fill Chocolate Log, or about 2 cups.

FRENCH CHOCOLATE FROSTING Melt chocolate and butter over hot water. Add sugar; blend well. Add milk and vanilla; pour slowly into chocolate mixture. Whisk until smooth. Makes enough to frost Chocolate Log, or about 1 cup.

Chocolate Treats Plain and Fancy, 1958

Funny Cake

INGREDIENTS

1¼ cups sifted cake flour
1 tsp. baking powder
½ tsp. salt
¾ cup sugar
¼ cup shortening or butter
½ cup milk
1 tsp. vanilla extract
1 egg
3 tbs. chopped nuts

BUTTERSCOTCH SAUCE
¼ cup butter
½ cup firmly packed brown sugar
2 tbs. light corn syrup
3 tbs. water
½ tsp. vanilla extract

DIRECTIONS

PREPARATIONS First, prepare a pastry mix or your favorite pastry. Roll ⅛ inch thick, fit into glass pie pan, and flute edge high.

BUTTERSCOTCH SAUCE
Combine butter, brown sugar, and light corn syrup in saucepan. Stir over low heat until mixture comes to a boil. Add water, bring again to a boil, and boil 1 to 2 minutes. Remove from heat. Add vanilla. Let cool to lukewarm while mixing this cake.

THE MIXING METHOD (Have all ingredients at room temperature.) Mix by hand or in electric mixer. Count only actual beating time or strokes. Scrape bowl and spoon or beater often.) Measure sifted flour into sifter; add baking powder, salt and sugar. Cream butter briefly. Add dry ingredients. Add milk and vanilla and mix until all flour is dampened. Then beat 2 minutes at a low speed of the mixer or 300 vigorous strokes by hand. Add egg and beat 2 minute longer or 150 strokes by hand. Pour batter in pastry liner pie pan. Pour the lukewarm sauce gently over batter and sprinkle with chopped nuts. Bake in a moderate oven (350°F) 50 to 55 minutes.

Cake is best served warm as dessert or as coffee cake. Top with whipped cream or ice cream for a special treat.

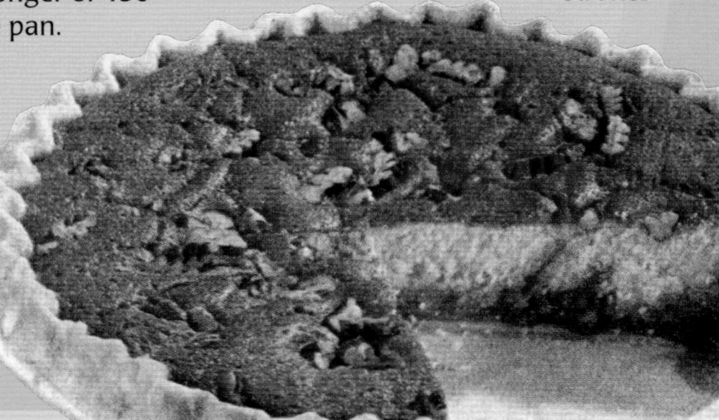

Cake Secrets, n.d.

LET'S Bake a cake